Songs of Chanukah

Compiled by Jeanne Modesitt

Illustrated by Robin Spowart

Musical Arrangements by Uri Ophir

Little, Brown and Company

Boston Toronto London

First Edition

Copyright acknowledgments appear on page 32

Library of Congress Cataloging-in-Publication Data

Songs of Chanukah / compiled by Jeanne Modesitt ; illustrated by Robin
Spowart ; musical arrangements by Uri Ophir. — 1st ed.
1 score.
Folk and contemporary songs.
For voice and piano; includes chord symbols for guitar.
English and Hebrew (romanized) words.
ISBN 0-316-57739-1
1. Hanukkah — Songs and music.   2. Jews — Music.   3. Folk music.
4. Folk-songs, Hebrew.   5. Songs, Hebrew.   I. Modesitt, Jeanne.
II. Spowart, Robin.   III. Ophir, Uri.
M2110.S599   1992   90-27455

10 9 8 7 6 5 4 3 2 1

WOR

Published simultaneously in Canada
by Little, Brown & Company (Canada) Limited

Printed in the United States of America

Contents

Chanukah Blessings

All around the world, when the eight-day holiday of Chanukah comes, candles are lit at sunset in Jewish homes. The candles are placed from right to left in a nine-branched candleholder called a *hanukkiyah*. The *shamash* (a helper candle) is used to light the other candles. On the first night, the *shamash* lights one candle, on the second night, two, on the third, three, until on the eighth night, all nine candles are burning brightly. (The candles are lit left to right, so that the last candle added is the first lit.)

As we light the candles, we sing or say the Chanukah blessings.

Blessed art Thou, Adonai our God, Ruler of the Universe,
Who has commanded us to kindle the Chanukah light.
Blessed art Thou, Adonai our God, Ruler of the Universe,
Who has wrought miracles for our ancestors
At this season in days of old.

Blessed art Thou, Adonai our God, Ruler of the Universe,
Who has kept us in life and has sustained us
And enabled us to reach this season.

Hanerot Halalu
(We Kindle These Lights)

This song, which traditionally follows the candle blessings, speaks about the holiness of Chanukah lights. As we look into the flames, we give thanks to God for all that the Holy One has given us and continues to give us.

We kindle these lights
For the wonders and the redemptions
Thou didst perform for our ancestors
Through Thy holy priests.
These Chanukah lights are holy,
And through them we sanctify Thy name.

Ma-oz Tzur
(Rock of Ages)

Over 2,000 years ago, Jews lived in the land of Judea (now called Israel), which was ruled by kings from other lands. When the Syrian king Antiochus came to rule Judea as part of the Greek Empire, he ordered Jews to give up their religion and follow the Greek religion instead. Some Jews obeyed the king, but many others did not. These brave men, women, and children refused to give up what they believed to be right. What heroes they were! This song praises God for the strength and courage the Holy One gave us when faced with those who wished to destroy us. The singing of the song traditionally closes the candle-lighting ceremony.

Rock of ages, let our song
Praise Thy saving power.
Thou amidst the raging foes
Wast our sheltering tower.
Furious they assailed us,
But Thine arm availed us.
(And Thy word broke their sword
When our own strength failed us.) *2x*

Y'mey HaChanukah
(O Chanukah)

A menorah is a seven-branched lamp stand that is a symbol of Jewish faith. A Chanukah menorah, a *hanukkiyah*, has nine branches. In some families, everyone lights his or her own *hanukkiyah*. In other families, people take turns lighting the candles.

The horah is a folk dance that is performed in a linked circle. It is a joyous dance — just right for Chanukah!

O Chanukah, O Chanukah, come light the menorah.
Let's have a party; we'll all dance the horah.
Gather round the table; we'll give you a treat.
Shiny tops to play with and pancakes to eat.
And while we are playing,
The candles are burning low.
(One for each night, they shed a sweet light,
To remind us of days long ago.) *2x*

O Chanukah, O Chanukah, a festival of joy.
A holiday, a jolly day for every girl and boy.
Spin the whirling dreydl all week long.
Eat the sizzling latkes; sing the happy songs.
Now light them tonight then,
The flickering candles in a row.
(Retell the wondrous story of God in all His glory,
And dance by the candles' cheering glow.) *2x*

Eight Candles

King Antiochus was very angry at the Jews who refused to obey his orders to give up their religion. He sent his troops into Judea. They tore up the inside of the great Temple (the center for Jews' worship), destroyed homes, and killed many Jews. Led first by Mattathias, and then Judah, a small band of Jewish farmers, shepherds, and teachers began to fight against the king's army. This band, later to be known as the Maccabees, had no experience as soldiers, very few weapons, and were ten times smaller in number than the king's army. But they believed in what they were doing — fighting for religious freedom — and this belief gave them strength, courage, and hope.

Eight candles shine for the Maccabees.
Eight candles shine for the Maccabees.
The tyrant was routed with all of his men,
And the Temple made holy again. *(Chorus)*

Eight candles shine for the Maccabees.
Eight candles shine for the Maccabees.
Chanukah's children will never forget
The glory that shines for us yet. *(Chorus)*

13

Eight Days of Chanukah

After three years of winning battle after battle against Antiochus's army, the Maccabees finally reached Jerusalem and reconquered it. When they saw what the army had done to the Temple, they wept. But soon after, the Maccabees and the villagers went to work: they scrubbed the Temple, threw out the Greek idols, and made a new menorah. On the twenty-fifth day of the month of Kislev (the month in the Jewish calendar that falls roughly in November/December), the Jews lit the menorah and rededicated the Temple to God. For eight days they celebrated joyfully. It was then decreed that Jews should celebrate these days every year, so that the story of the Maccabees, the triumph of right over might, would never be forgotten.

And what about the jar of oil the song speaks of? According to legend, when the Jews rededicated the Temple and were about to light the menorah, they found only one jug of sealed, pure oil — enough to last for just one day. But instead the oil burned for eight days. It was a miracle!

Mi Y'maleil
(Who Can Retell)

Throughout history, Jews have been persecuted for their religion. Even today, there are some lands in which Jews are not permitted to openly celebrate Jewish holidays, pray in synagogues, or attend Hebrew schools. Many of these Jews, however, celebrate their holidays and study their Hebrew texts in secret. How courageous they are! In remembrance of these Jews, some people light an extra menorah each night of Chanukah.

Who can retell the things that befell us?
Who can count them?
In every age a hero or sage
Came to our aid.
Hark! At this time of year in days of yore,
Maccabees the Temple did restore.
And today our people as we dreamed
Will arise, unite, and be redeemed.

Lichvod HaChanukah
(Because It's Chanukah)

Latkes, or potato pancakes, are traditional Chanukah treats because they are made with oil and remind us of the miracle of the jug of oil that burned for eight days.

Father lights the Chanukah candles.
(The *shamash* burns so bright.) *2x*
(Do you know why he lights them?) *3x*
Because it's Chanukah.

Mother bakes the potato latkes.
(Latkes so warm and sweet.) *2x*
(Do you know why she bakes them?) *3x*
Because it's Chanukah.

Levivot
(Chanukah Pancakes)

"Chanukah's latkes teach us that one cannot live by miracles alone." (folk proverb)

RECIPE FOR LATKES

4 large potatoes (3 pounds)	⅓ cup flour or matzoh meal
1 small onion	1 tsp. salt
2 eggs	oil for frying

Grate potatoes and onion and place in bowl. Drain off excess liquid. Add eggs, flour, and salt. Over medium heat, drop mixture by quarter cupfuls into well-oiled frying pan. Fry on both sides until golden brown. Serve with applesauce, yogurt, or sour cream. Makes 16 latkes.

Words by L. Kipnis

Music by N. Nardi

Ke- mach, ke- mach
Ke- mach, ke- mach

min ha- sak, She- men, she- men min ha- kad. Cha- nu- kah ha- yom, —
min ha- sak, She- men, she- men min ha- kad. Ha- va ne- la- bev, —

1. Chag na- im nech- mad. —

2. le- vi- vot le- chag. La, la, la, la, la, la,

la, la, la, la, la, la, la, la, la, la, la, la, la, la, la, la, la, la, la, la, la, la, la, la, la,

la, la, la, la, la, la, la. (fine)

Bring the flour from the bin;
Pour the oil from the tin.
Chanukah is here, festival so dear.

Mix the flour snowy white,
With the oil so golden bright.
That's how mother makes Chanukah pancakes.
La, la, la . . .

S'vivon
(Little Spinning Top)

S'vivon is the Hebrew word for dreydl. A dreydl is a small spinning top with four sides. Each side has a Hebrew letter. The letters stand for the words *Nes gadol haya sham,* which means "A great miracle happened there." On an Israeli dreydl, one letter is different — the letters stand for *Nes gadol haya poh,* "A great miracle happened here." Have you ever danced like a dreydl? It's fun!

S'vivon, turn and turn,
While the lovely candles burn.
What a wondrous holiday;
Watch us sing and dance and play.
Tell the story full of cheer:
A great miracle happened there.
It's a holiday of light
For eight days and eight nights.

I Have a Little Dreydl

HOW TO PLAY DREYDL

Players start with an equal number of objects (such as nuts, pennies, or raisins). Each player puts one object in the middle, or the pot. Everyone takes turn spinning the dreydl. If the dreydl lands on

- נ Nun: the player does nothing
- ג Gimel: the player takes everything in the pot
- ה He: the player takes half the pot (or half plus one extra if there is an odd number in the pot)
- ש Shin: the player puts one object in the pot

Whenever the pot is empty, or there is only one object left in it, each player has to put one object in before the next spin. When one player has all the objects, the game is over and ready to begin again!

Words by S. Grossman

Music by S. Goldfarb

It has a lovely body, with a leg so short and thin.
And when it is all tired, it drops and then I win. *(Chorus)*
My dreydl's always playful; it loves to dance and spin.
A happy game of dreydl, come play, now let's begin. *(Chorus)*

Chanukah Chag Yafe
(Chanukah, A Happy Holiday)

Along with eating special foods, story telling, singing, and game playing, many Jews also exchange gifts during Chanukah. Some people give gifts on the first night, others on the last; still others give gifts on all eight nights. Sometimes children also receive *Chanukah gelt,* or Chanukah money. The amounts are always small, usually a few coins. Because Chanukah is a time for *tzedakah* — helping those in need — children are encouraged to set aside some of their Chanukah gelt to put in the *tzedakah* box at home or school.

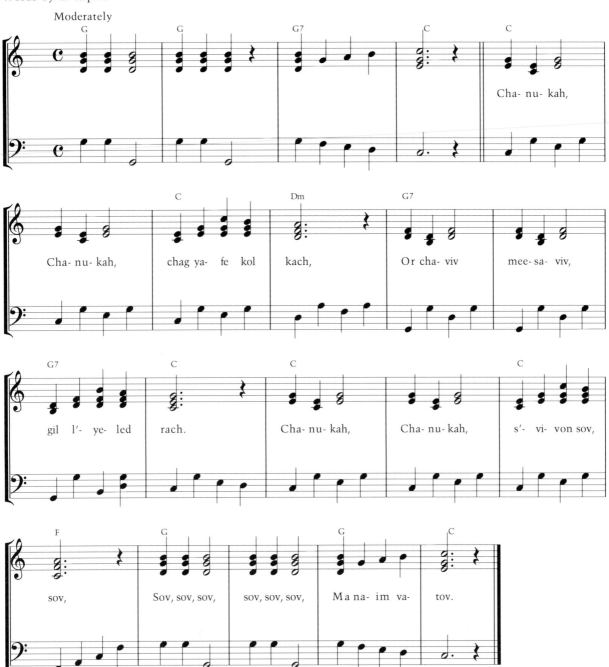

Chanukah, Chanukah, happy holiday,
Candles bright, cheerful light,
Old and young are gay.
Chanukah, Chanukah, *s'vivon sov, sov,*
Spin and turn, spin and turn,
While the candles burn.

Ner Li
(Tiny Candle)

Many people place their lit menorahs by a window facing the street. This way, passersby can see the lights and know that the people inside are celebrating Chanukah.

Words by L. Kipnis
English verse by S. Gewirtz

Music by D. Sambursky

There's a tiny candle glowing through the night.
Shining at the window it brings a special light.
(On Chanukah it seems to say,
"Thank you, O Lord, for this special day.") *2x*

Burn, Little Candles

Chanukah is a celebration of miracles. As we watch the candles burn, we are reminded of the miracle of the Maccabees' victory over the Syrian army and their rededication of the Temple. We are reminded of the miracle of the oil that burned for eight days. And we are reminded that miracles continue to happen today and will for the rest of time.

Words and music by R. Cook

Shine, lit- tle can- dles, burn- ing bright;
Dance, lit- tle can- dles, to and fro,

Cha- nu- kah is here.
Stand- ing tall and bright.

Eight lit- tle can- dles
Dance, lit- tle can- dles

in a row
in a row;

With a flame so clear.
Dance for all eight nights.

Melt, little candles, one by one;
You have been such fun.
Eight little candles go to sleep
When Chanukah is done.

31